Sanity Savers
for Moms

Sanity Savers
for Moms

7 Simple Solutions for a More Joy-filled Life

Kristi Clover

Dedication

This book is dedicated to my amazing husband, Steve. I'm so blessed to be married to you. Thanks for being on this crazy adventure of parenting with me. You help bring me sanity. Thanks for all your love, support, and encouragement as I pursue my dreams. You are my favorite half!

Special Thanks

Grant & Blake Clover: You two are amazing sons! Thank you so much for all the babysitting you did in the final days of this book. You both are such awesome helpers and so patient with your younger siblings. I could not be more proud of the incredible, young men you have become! I love you so much!

Cynthia Zarcone: Thank you for the late night editing and feedback that helped bring continuity to the book and focus to my creativity. You are such a wonderful blessing to me.

◎ About the Author ◎

Kristi is a Christian, homeschooling mom to five blessings ranging from teens to tots and wife to her high school crush. Aside from her family, she's passionate about encouraging and inspiring women in their daily lives as moms, wives, and homeschoolers by offering "Simple Solutions for a More Joy-filled Life."

Not surprisingly, you can usually find her at home trying to bring some order and fun into the mayhem of daily life. Kristi is a speaker, author, and blogger. She loves to share insights from her wonderful, yet sometimes challenging, experiences of being a homemaker and homeschool mom.

Her tips are creative, practical, and help bring back some simplicity in the chaos of life and homeschooling—helping moms to let go of the mommy guilt they often feel in this "Pinterest-perfect" world. She blogs about her adventures in wifehood, mommyhood, and the fun to be found in homeschooling at KristiClover.com.

You can find her on YouTube, Facebook, and Pinterest as @RaisingClover and on Instagram, Twitter, and Periscope as @KristiClover. She's also the author of The Scoop on Scope: Periscope Pointers for Beginners, Bloggers, and Beyond!

It's Finally Here!!

The Simply Joyful Podcast! A podcast focused on "simply joyful" living in all the various roles moms play each day: faith building, parenting, homemaking, homeschooling,—& more! Listen in and find out more at

www.simplyjoyfulpodcast.com

KristiClover.com

Live Simply. Be Joyful.

Contents

❂ Introduction ❂

Welcome to Sanity

From "Dark Days" to Joy!

Attaining sanity in the midst of motherhood sometimes seems like an impossible task. Motherhood by definition is often a bit chaotic. Of course, there are days when "a bit chaotic" is "a bit of" an understatement. We've all had those days.

I went through a season several years ago that I refer to as *"my dark days."* We had so much insanity happening all around us that sometimes all I could do was just keep putting one foot in front of the other and pray God would get me through—while tears streamed down my face. I couldn't see any light at the end of the tunnel.

At the time I only had two little boys, and by little I mean 20 months old and 3 months old. We had just moved away from my family and our good friends in northern California and bought a house in San Diego, and **everything that could have gone wrong pretty much did go wrong—and then some!**

I can look back and laugh now. Honestly, it was like being in a sitcom where it was one crazy thing after another happening to the poor main character—I just happened to be that poor main character. *I am so thankful to have those days behind me, yet through it all I really did learn so much.*

It was during those hard times that I realized that something had to give, so I learned to quickly prioritize everything we were doing. *This is also the point at which I learned that I could not survive any longer without order.*

So, I read just about every article or book that I could get my hands on about organizing. I asked all my organized friends for advice and tips for those tough-to-stay-clean areas. Do you know what I discovered? **I had a real knack for figuring out how to simplify what I was learning. I call it "gleaning and tweaking."** I learned to "glean" from the information I was reading and getting from others and "tweak" it to make it simpler and a better fit for our family.

Through the years I have tried a variety of different systems in my home to *bring some order to the chaos of our days.* Some things have worked, others haven't. We've also added more chaos by way of adding three more children to the mix since my "dark days"—and we started homeschooling several years ago.

I guess I just want you to understand that I get it. I don't live in a "Pinterest perfect" world, nor do I try to. I believe that it's important for moms to be real with each other. It's a blessing! However, reality means life can be stressful and messy. Some days can bring you to the brink of insanity—hence, the inspiration for this book.

I pray that this little book will bless you and help to equip you with a few tools to bring you a little extra joy and sanity. This book is also meant to be a little taste of what you'll find on my blog: KristiClover.com. I hope you'll join me there. I want to give you a sense of my heart for encouraging moms just like you to find "simple solutions for a more joy-filled life."

Blessings & joy,

Kristi Clover

I have a TON of recommendations and resources included in this book. I do list most of them at the end of each chapter. However, I created a **Sanity Savers Resources** page on my blog for you to have everything all in one place along with links and a few extra book recommendations. Be sure to check it out:

KristiClover.com/SanitySaversResources

Want to get all the great Printables?

Reading this on Kindle or in Print?

I'd love for you to be able to actually "print" these fun printables. I have them available for you (and so much more) when you join my "Simply Joyful" community.

Go to:

KristiClover.com/SanitySaversPrintables

◎ Chapter One ◎

SANITY SAVER #1

Eliminate Morning Mayhem!

Life seems to just keep getting crazier and crazier on every front. A good morning can make all the difference in whether you have a "smooth sailing" kind of day or a "stormy, tossed overboard" kind of day.

When my kids went to traditional school, it was the typical mad dash to get kids up, dressed, fed, lunches packed, baby nursed, backpacks ready, and SHOES on! (I can't tell you how many times we'd show up at school to discover that one child had forgotten to put his shoes on.)

We may not be racing out the door every morning like we used to, but *mornings still have a tendency to get derailed if I'm not intentional with how I plan for them.*

I find that if I let things get too "loosey-goosey" in the mornings, then our whole day gets thrown off. Whenever I feel like our mornings are getting out-of-whack, the first thing I do is ask myself, "What is causing my mornings to be so crazy?" Then I devise a plan of attack. Most "morning fails" can be solved by following the same basic game plan:

4 Simple Tips For A More Joy-Filled Morning!

#1 Plan & Prepare the Night Before!

There is really no better way to have a great morning than by starting the night before! Planning ahead is the key! My two top priorities for my mornings—besides greeting each member of my family with a smile, kiss, and hug—are to get time in the Word and time for some exercise. ***One key to achieving these two goals is how well I've planned and prepared the night before***.

Planning

The first thing I do each night is to take a *look at my calendar and figure out when the best time will be* for me to have my quiet time and get my workout in. I even go as far as to formulate a "back-up plan" just in case my morning gets hijacked by my littles. I know there will be "those days" when it doesn't seem to matter how early I've gotten up or how well I've planned out my mornings. I'm completely convinced that there must be an invisible "trip alarm" that goes off in my kids' rooms whenever I try to wake up early to get a jump on the day. It never fails that I'll have a little one calling to me from the monitor or sleepily walking down the stairs to greet me.

Prepping

The next important part of my evening routine is to set out things that I know I'll need to streamline my morning. I make sure to have my Bible and journal out along with a pen and a few index cards, so I'm ready for my quiet time. I also lay out my workout clothes and shoes in a spot where I can quickly change into them in the morning. This is so helpful in getting me out the door (especially if I'm trying not to wake anyone up as I sneak out for my morning walk or run). I've even noticed that setting out cereal bowls the night before helps me get breakfast on the table more efficiently.

If we have to rush out the door early the next day, I'll get everything set for us to grab-and-go along with a list of last minute items I don't want to forget to bring. When I know my mornings are well-planned, I'm more relaxed and less stressed out—even on those mornings we are racing out the door to catch an early flight with my family of seven. **When we plan ahead, there are fewer tantrums by toddlers—and mommy!**

#2 Get to bed early!

If you really want to start your day off the best you can, then you have to get to bed early. We are essentially working backwards here: We are starting at the end of "yesterday" to have a smooth "today." We haven't even gotten to morning and already I've talked about two things that need to be done before your morning starts. Ha! I guess the best way to put this is that it's best to start before you fail, so you don't fail before you start!

Start before you fail, so you don't fail before you start!

As you are about to see, my tip #3 is to get up early. It's easier to wake up early when you've gotten enough sleep. The best way to figure out what time you need to get yourself to bed is to *determine what time you want to get up and how many hours of sleep you'd like to get*. These days I'm trying to get up at 6am. I know that I need at least 7 hours of sleep to function properly. This means I have to get myself in bed no later than 11pm. It's really hard to move onto the next tip without encouraging this one. I will admit that when push comes to shove and I have writing deadlines—well, I tend to stay up late to write. That's my "fringe" time. Crazy thing is that I still try to be up by 6:30am. Those are the mornings I'm so grateful we invested in a Keurig. I definitely don't keep myself on this "sleep deprived" schedule for too long, because I know I'll burn out. I do need my sleep, otherwise I'm no good to anyone. I actually try to get naps on these "lack of sleep" days. I admit all this to you, so you know that I completely understand that life has seasons when it is hard to set bedtimes for yourself.

Sleep is important to sanity! *Sleep deprivation is a form of torture*. So, don't torture yourself with bad sleep habits.

Evening Goals:

- Plan! Check your calendar and make a plan (even a back-up)!
- Prepare! Prep everything that you'll need for your smooth morning!
- Get to Bed! Go to bed early enough to get the sleep you'll need for your early start!

#3 Get up early!

There is no better way to eliminate morning craziness than to get a jump on your morning! There are so many books written all about the importance of getting up early. As a mom, this is especially important. Personally, if I can just get a little time in the Word *before my kids get up*, then I'm a changed woman for the day.

Like I already mentioned, my goal is to get up and go for a walk, have a nice long devotion, and get my shower done all before the kids get up—but that's not always realistic. *So, I prioritize! I figure out what is most important for me to get done before our morning kicks off* (and I have a toddler glued to me). I'll be sharing about my "4F's" in chapter 5, but you'll see that my priority is to have time with the Lord first! I set my Bible out in a nice little spot (like I mentioned above) and prioritize that time in the morning.

Know this: as a mom of five, I completely understand that this is easier said than done when you have little ones with unpredictable sleep schedules. You may be in a season right now when your baby or little one (or two) keep you up late or up throughout the night, or they may just wake up crazy early (like my kids do). That all makes it hard to get up early. However, I still think it's really important to try—sometimes you have to get creative to make it happen.

When I had newborns and was up a couple times during the night to feed them, I'd often have my devotion time as I nursed in the wee hours of the morning. When I was done feeding the baby, I'd go back to sleep. *So, I was getting my time in the Word, it just looked different. This is where creating a plan works well.*

"She gets up before dawn to prepare breakfast for her household and plan the day's work for her servant girls."

Proverbs 31:15

#4 Have More Accountability for Your Kids

I have done a horrible job in the past at following up with my kids to see if they have done their devotions, brushed their teeth, practiced piano, picked up their rooms, and finished their other morning responsibilities. *Our day gets moving, and things just get missed.* It's kind of a domino effect— for me and the rest of the family. *If I don't follow up and have routines in order, then everything starts falling apart.*

Incorporating "accountability" into our morning routine is key for helping me to not lose my cool with my kids when things are forgotten or missed. It's so easy to get frustrated when your kids just don't seem to be consistent at getting through their "to-do" list in the morning. *I've found that setting a deadline for when I expected the work to be completed—and actually checking up on whether things got done—gave me so much more peace throughout the day.*

Bonus tip: I love using a whiteboard to jot things down that I see still need to be completed. When I write it down and my kids know where to check, there is less frustration and better communication.

Other Resources

- **Printable**
  —Be sure to check out the printable I created to help you create your own morning routine in Chapter 9.

- **Online**
  —Make Over Your Mornings by Crystal Paine of Money Saving Mom is a great program to help you transform your mornings.

  —DIY Breakfast Stations by Kim Sorgius of Not Consumed is a fabulous way to get breakfast underway in the mornings.

- **Pinterest**
  —Check out my Pinterest board called "Food Yums for Breakfast!" Hopefully, you'll find some yummy inspirations for breakfast.

*Links to all of these resources are found at:

KristiClover.com/SanitySaversResources

◎ Chapter Two ◎

SANITY SAVER #2

Create Routine!

I'm not a huge fan of schedules. I do use schedules for some things, but I don't run my house on a schedule. I prefer routines. ***Creating routines helps with just about anything!*** I sometimes refer to this as "getting your groove on!" When you repeat your daily routines over and over each day, it helps you to find a flow for your day, form new habits, and get into a "groove."

Bad habits can be broken with new routines!

For me this rang true with my sunglasses dilemma. I was constantly losing my sunglasses. I'd have them on my head when I'd walk in the house, then heaven only knows where they'd end up after that. I'd set them down in the kitchen or upstairs somewhere. We'd be backing out of the driveway when I'd realize that they weren't in my purse. I'd then go running around (making us late) trying to find them. I was driving my husband crazy!

If you have a particularly bad habit you are trying to get on top of, simply break it down into what you think would be the best "step-by-step" solution— and implement it! Don't be afraid to "tweak" the process a few times to get it just right. As for the sunglasses example, I now I have a routine. When I come in the door, I put my keys on the hook, hang my purse up, place my glasses in their case (novel ideas, I know), and put the case back in my purse. I also take my cell phone out of my purse and set it on the counter in the kitchen. This little "coming in the door" routine has saved me so many headaches. Now I always know my glasses are in their case. The nice, little bonus is that my cell phone doesn't stay lost in my big purse where I can't hear it when I get a text or call.

You may be wondering, "What's the difference between schedules and routines?" *Well, the simple answer is that it all boils down to how you divide up your time.*

Schedules...

Typically, with a schedule you are dividing up time into "time slots."

- 7am-Get up
- 7:15am-Eat breakfast
- 7:30am-Shower
- 7:45am-Devotions...etc.

This is how most planners are set up. I used to love schedules. I had my entire day planned out with precision. The only problem was if anything new needed to be added to my day or if we got at all off track, then my whole schedule was thrown off. I spent most days feeling behind and overwhelmed—and trying desperately to get back on track and on schedule. Stress! I found myself totally irritable and crabby with my kids. In my mind they were to blame for my pretty, little schedule being off course. Not my finest hours.

Routines...

Routines are a bit different. I've found so much more grace and peace using routines! *I divide my routines into "blocks of time" throughout the day. There is so much more flexibility for life (and grace for my kids)—plus I find that I'm not watching the clock all day.*

The way I set up my routines is to figure out what I want to have accomplished in each segment of our day:

- Morning Routine (7am-9am): Breakfast, get dressed, devotions, piano, brush teeth, and morning chores.
- Afternoon (11:30-1:30pm): Lunch, outdoor time, sibling play time (this is the one-on-one play time that I rotate between my older kids with their younger siblings, so my other kids have some quiet to finish up their school work while another sibling is playing with the littles), and a quick clean up time.
- Nap time and Quiet time (2-4pm): Writing or errand time for me.
- Evening (6-8:30pm): Family devotion and prayer, PJs, brush and floss teeth, bedtime—and, of course, next day prep.

It's so much easier for me to train my kids to know what their morning routines are rather than telling them what to do next every 15 minutes. When I say, "Let's get our morning routine done," they know what they need to get accomplished. Okay, there is still a lot of reminding that happens, but I don't get stressed out when they are a few minutes behind on a particular chore.

Notice there are gaps in our routine time frames. That's when we do our homeschooling and other activities. This just creates a framework for me for when I want to get certain aspects of our daily "to-do's" done.

I have routines for just about everything we do, whether it's when we get laundry done, the dish washer unloaded, tidy up the house, and more. We have routines that we follow that help everyone to accomplish things more efficiently.

Other Resources:

- **Posts**

    —I have a series on my blog called "M.O.M.=Master Organizers of Mayhem" (I'm hoping to eventually turn it into a book). Here are a few posts that add more details as to how to create a great routine:

    M.O.M. Rule # 3: Get Your Groove On!

    M.O.M. Rule # 8: Don't Start From Scratch—"Glean & Tweak!"

    *Links to all of these resources are found at:

    KristiClover.com/SanitySaversResources

Chapter Three

SANITY SAVER #3

Keep Your Knees Dirty!

Life is messy when you're a mom. We deal with "dirty" all day long. Whether it's dirty diapers, dirty dishes, dirty clothes, dirty hands, dirty whatever, dirt is a daily part of motherhood.

When I say we need to "keep our knees dirty," I'm not talking about the kneeling we do as we are scrubbing floors or toilets. I'm referring to our need for prayer. We don't always have to "literally" be on our knees to pray, *we just need to remember to get our "spiritual" knees dirty every day—all day*.

We all need to make time for the Word and prayer! I know some mornings don't lend themselves to one hour Bible study time. Exhaustion can also make it difficult to get up early to get in the Word. However, *I try to remind myself that I'm too busy NOT to pray and find time to read my Bible. I need His strength to help me throughout the day*. I need to slow down enough to be able to hear His still, small voice. I need time to refocus my mind on His desires for me, my family, and my day—not mine.

His Strength, Not Ours...

Have you ever gone through a hard time or just been completely overwhelmed and had someone try to encourage you with, "God will never give you more than you can handle." I've been hearing that for years. The verse that is getting misquoted is 1 Corinthians 10:13 and it says "God will not let you be *tempted* beyond what you can bear" (emphasis is mine). He does give us more than we can handle! He does it all the time. He specializes in it—because in our weakness, He shows Himself strong *(2 Corinthians 12:9-10).

There is no way you or I can do all that God is calling us to do as moms in our own strength. The faster we realize this and draw on Him for strength, the faster He'll supply it and bring His joy and peace. I really love what 2 Corinthians 1:8-11 says about relying on God. It talks about how "we are under great pressure, far beyond our ability to endure....this happens that we might not rely on ourselves but on God,..." The best way to rely on Him is to set our hearts and minds on Him and His Word. Whether you are physically getting on your knees and praying or just praying as you go about your day, we need to ask God for His strength and trust Him to supply it.

"Blessed is the man who trusts in the Lord, whose confidence is in Him. He will be like a tree planted by the water that sends out its roots by the stream. It does not fear when heat comes; its leaves are always green. It has no worries in a year of drought and never fails to bear fruit."

(Jeremiah 17: 7,8)

This is one of my favorite verses. It makes me stop and think about whether I've sent my "roots" deep enough each day to draw on Him so that I can bear fruit in my home.

Finding Time for Prayer

We don't have enough strength to endure all that this crazy world will throw at us this side of heaven. When things are most chaotic that's the time I feel God is saying, "You need to spend a little more time with me." Sometimes I'll go shut myself in my room—even if this means that I have to put a video on for the kids. We have to spend time with the Lord. It's the only way to make it through the overwhelming seasons that life and motherhood can bring.

Time "on our knees" is the only way to make it through the overwhelming seasons that life and motherhood can bring.

I try not to even get out of bed without praying. It's hard on those mornings when you've been woken up by a screaming child—however, prayer is even more necessary on those days.

Sometimes I will leave my Bible open on the counter as I'm making breakfast or brushing my teeth to get a little time in the Word. Yes, I know it is best to actually pull away in solitude for prayer—but we're moms. Solitude doesn't happen all the time. I try to find quiet moments when I can pray, like when everyone's eating. I might walk out of the room for a bit of prayer time.

I also like to pick a piece of Scripture to mediate on throughout the day. I try to jot it down on an index card or sticky note to keep with me or post in a prominent place. Other times I'll just leave my Bible open to that verse or pulled up on my Bible app. This way no matter what I'm doing—I'm praying over that Scripture.

Here's a Few Simple Tips for Finding Time to Get in the Word

- **Keep your Bible open!** It always helps me to sneak a little extra time in the Word when I leave my Bible open in the room I spend most of my day (like on the kitchen counter).
- **Get a good Bible app!** Be sure to download a Bible app or two for your phone or tablet. My favorites are the Blue Letter Bible app and the YouVersion Bible app.
- **Use your "Quiet Time!"** Dedicate some of your "quiet time" or "nap time" to having a quiet time with the Lord. (We'll talk more about "quiet" time in chapter 6.)
- **Read a psalm and a proverb first thing in the morning!**
- **Write it out!** If you have an extra minute or two, write out a verse that really stuck out to you on an index card and stick it where you can meditate on it for the day.
- **Plan for it!** Look at your day and figure out when the best time to fit it in would be—then make it part of your routine.
- **Listen to the Word!** Listen to an audio version of the Bible with your ear buds in while you go about your day, are off running errands, or out for a walk.
- **Get your kids busy!** Get your kids busy with something—even if it's watching a video—and get your nose in the Word.

- **"Read before you feed!"** One of my favorite tricks to get myself to "feed" on His Daily Bread first thing in the morning is to not allow myself to eat physical food until I've "eaten" spiritual food. I definitely get into the Word on the days I give myself this rule.
- **Bookend your day!** It's a great idea to bookend your day in the Word and in prayer—morning and evening.

Other Resources:

- **Apps**
  —Blue Letter Bible app and YouVerse Bible app

- **Websites**
  —Blue Letter Bible and Bible Gateway

- **Movies**
  —Rent the movie "War Room" to be inspired!

- **Post**
  —I wrote a post called When Things Go Squish in the Night that you might enjoy.

*Links to all of these resources are found at:

KristiClover.com/SanitySaversResources

☮ *Chapter Four* ☮

SANITY SAVER #4

Simplify!

There are so many choices to make in a day, and usually not enough time to say "yes" to everything thrown at you. It's easy to over-schedule and over-commit ourselves—and our family. I've had to work really hard at saving my "yes's" for only the very best things. Nothing creates more chaos in the home than an overly busy schedule. There are obviously busy seasons in life. However, these days it seems to be the trend to cram-pack our calendars with activities and commitments. If you are spending more time in your car shuttling people from one thing to the next or not finding time for regular meals at the table as a family, then I'd encourage you to re-evaluate your schedule.

THIS IS VERY HARD! I hate saying "no" to things. It has been a very difficult process for our family as we pulled out of some ministries, sports, and other involvements to make sure we had time for our family. Ministries and other service opportunities are a great way to serve the Lord and others, but God wants your family to be your #1 ministry! This doesn't get you out of serving. Serving others is awesome, but not if you are constantly sacrificing family time. Sometimes, this also means that not every kid is in a sport at the same time and we don't do some of the fun activities that we used to do (at least not at the same time). There is just not enough time in the day!

Simplifying is so vital to your family's ability to thrive. It's a hard thing to do, but slowing down is so important! Learning to pick only the very best things takes time. There have been times when I've committed to helping with a project, and part of the way through the process I realize that I probably bit off more than I could chew. I try not to beat myself up over it, but I do make sure to do a better job of evaluating a commitment the next time something comes up.

Simplifying is so vital to your family's ability to thrive.

Prioritizing

When I need help prioritizing my family's time, I use a little "Four-Leaf" approach to things.

I call it my "4F's:" Faith, Family, Friends, and Fellowman. Following these priorities in this order helps me to make decisions about how to best simplify our lives.

The "4 F's"

Faith * Family * Friends * Fellowman

Digging Deeper

I like to think of simplifying as embracing a "Mary" mentality in a "Martha" Stewart world! If you are not familiar with the story of Mary and Martha in Luke 10:38-42, I'll explain it here. Jesus and His disciples were visiting the home of Martha. While Martha was busying herself with getting everything ready, her sister Mary sat at Jesus's feet and listened to what He was saying. The Bible actually says that Martha was "distracted by all the preparations that had to be made" (verse 40). Let me stop here for a moment to say, "Wow!" I can totally relate to Martha. I love entertaining and hosting people in my home. There is a lot to get done, so I can understand her busyness.

To continue with the story, Martha gets upset at her sister and asks Jesus to tell her sister to get up and help her. Well, Jesus's response in this verse has been life changing for me, "'Martha, Martha,'" the Lord answered, "'you are worried and upset about many things, but only one thing is needed. Mary has chosen what is better, and it will not be taken away from her'" (Luke 10:41-42). Martha was distracted. She was worried. She was upset.

How like Martha I can be on a daily basis. My day gets underway, my kids are bustling about, and I have a to-do list that isn't going to take care of itself. I'm Martha. Now, we all need to have a little Martha in us or nothing gets done—but not at the expense of time with the Lord! We have to choose "what is better" and not allow anything else in our day to take us from our time with Jesus. We need to stop, sit at His feet, and listen.

I try daily to choose what is better! What's best! It's not always easy. If I'm not intentional about getting my time in the Word, then it doesn't always happen (like I talked about in chapter 1). If I allow too many things in our schedule or take on more than I can chew for my day, I tend to start dropping balls—sometimes the wrong balls (as my friend Colleen Kessler would say).

My Tips for Simplifying

#1 Reset your expectations!

There are just seasons when you have to lower your expectations of what you are able to get done—especially when you have a new baby or you homeschool. When it comes to homemaking, what helped me was to sit down with my husband and figure out what was most important to him for me to get done around the house. I discovered that his priorities are clean counters and dinner planned out. Knowing this helps me to focus on getting those two things done first—and took a ton of pressure off of me to get everything done. {I do clean more than just the counters. I don't want you calling health services on me.}

#2 Make a list!

I do a basic brain dump of everything we have going on. After we have our list complete, my husband and I sit down and do a simple "A.B.C." prioritizing. This helps me to know what has to stay on our calendar and what we can take off.

A=Absolutely
B=Better try to keep
C=Can live without

#3 Just say, "No!"

I'm a people pleaser by nature, so I love to say "yes." It makes me happy to bless people with my "yes." The problem with this is that I'm ultimately not blessing my family nor myself if I'm saying "yes" to too many things. I know I've already said this, but save your "yes" for only the *very best things*!

#4 Declutter!

Okay, so decluttering is a whole big "can of worms" to get into in one little sub-point in a book. Ha! I just can't talk about simplifying without talking about all the "stuff" that fills our homes to overflow. So, I'll try to "simplify" my technique here. Just know that nothing creates more insanity than clutter!! Clutter=Chaos!

Now don't laugh, but before I start to declutter, I pray. Really, I do! I pray for God to help me be ruthless as I sort through things. *I pray for strength to say good-bye to things that are creating clutter and stress and interfering with my ability to manage my home and my time better for Him.* I also ask for vision for each room. By this I mean that I might spend time at the end of my "purge" moving furniture around for better function, or even have an idea for something new to put on the wall to make the room more inviting and bless those who enter the room. *God blesses our work when we invite Him to be a part of it.*

The simple way of explaining how I approach decluttering is that I go room-by-room and create four piles. Sometimes I use laundry baskets to help me sort, other times I just use sticky notes in front of my piles to keep things straight.

My "Four-Leaf" Approach to Decluttering:

* Keep * Toss * Give Away * Sell

- **Keep!** I try to be very brutal with what I decide to put in the keep pile. These items are assigned a "home" and get put away as soon as my big sort is done.
- **Toss!** Trinket treasures, broken toys, and any small meaningless decor is really just "house dander" and belongs in the trash. You don't want it laying around. You only want really special things to be kept.
- **Give Away!** This will hopefully be a big pile. Remind yourself that you might be creating treasure for someone else with your no-longer-needed items. I used to waste so much time trying to organize

things that really just needed to find new homes or be tossed out.

- **Sell!** Now this pile is a dangerous pile!! I usually start with the wonderful intent to have a garage sale or put things on Craig's List. Give yourself a time frame for this—a goal! Otherwise, this pile needs to become a second trip to your favorite donation location.

Clearing out clutter always feels so good. Plus I get excited that I just kept myself from debuting in the next show of Hoarders. As you are clearing out your physical clutter in your home, keep in mind that a cluttered schedule counts as clutter, too. Going back to Tip #3, keep "sorting" and saying "no" to things that don't need to be cluttering your calendar. Don't just try to better organize things into your calendar or set-up more carpools, some things need to be "trashed/tossed."

Learning to simplify is an art. It takes time and practice. However, you and your family will be so blessed by the joy that will follow.

· Other Resources:

- **Post**
  —M.O.M. Rule #4 Clear the Clutter

- **Books**
  —*The Best Yes* by Lysa TerKeurst—I highly recommend checking this fabulous book out if you struggle with being too much of a "yes" person.

  —*The Life-Changing Magic of Tidying Up: The Japanese Art of Decluttering and Organizing* by Marie Kondo.

I've created a complete list of all the books mentioned in this book and more at:

KristiClover.com/SanitySaversResources

○ *Chapter Five* ○

SANITY SAVER #5

Your Crock Pot & Freezer = Your Best Friends!

"What's for dinner?" This is the thought that can haunt any woman. You've had a hard day and you just want to crash, but there are mouths to feed (again!). Well, the secret is out—your crock pot and your freezer should be your very best friends!

I'd be remiss if I didn't first mention that meal planning is a key component to relieving extra stress from mealtimes. It's helpful to have the ingredients on hand that you are going to throw into your crock pot. I have a post on my blog that goes through all my best meal planning tips (I linked it at the end of this chapter). Do note that I've included my "handy-dandy" meal planner and grocery list in the printables section of this book. You're going to love it! It is one of my most popular printables.

Meal planning is my secret to getting my hungry crew fed. *Meal planning that includes crock pot meals and freezer meals is my secret to sanity!*

Your Crock Pot...

I have all kinds of tips and tricks on how to meal plan and make quick and easy meals, however *my crock pot is my greatest weapon to combat the "what's cooking?" dilemma.*

Top Tips for Your Using Your Crock Pot

#1 Get in the habit of making breakfast and dinner together.

As I'm pulling breakfast items out for our morning, I'm also pulling all my dinner ingredients together for our evening. Some days I do this at lunch time and just cook the meal on high.

#2 Look through your current recipes.

You'd be surprised just how many of your own recipes can be made in a crock pot. I have found that a lot of my chicken recipes were easily transformed into crock pot meals. I make a lot of my soups in a crock pot instead of on my stove top, as well.

#3 Gather & store.

Start gathering great crock pot recipes and put them all in one easy spot so you can find them quickly. I suggest making two copies of crock pot recipes. I file one by ingredient (chicken, beef, etc) and the other in a "crock pot" file. This makes my life so much easier.

#4 Ask friends.

Don't be afraid to ask your friends for their crock pot recipes. I even hosted a recipe exchange party a few years ago where everyone brought copies of their family favorite recipes. It was so much fun to get a stack of tried-and-true meals. You could do this specifically with crock pot recipes, too. I've also sent emails out asking for recipes.

#5 Pinterest!

I love Pinterest as a source for getting great dinner ideas and new crock pot recipes to try. You can my look around my Pinterest boards or simply do a search for crock pot, slow cooker, or freezer meal recipes.

#6 My Website!

Ha! My love for crock pot recipes has made its way to my blog KristiClover.com. You can simply go to my "Food" tab and find all the recipes I've put on there.

Your Freezer...

Freezer meals are great for those crazy seasons in life. So, when I am expecting a busy season in my life, like morning sickness, bringing home a new baby, basketball season (with dinner time practices), or any other long period of chaos (like my recent surgery), *I plan a big freezer meal prep day*. I gather my "go-to" recipes, make a big shopping list, have my hubby watch kids, and then I just go for it!

One awesome way I get freezer meals done is to simply double the recipe as I'm making one for dinner. It doesn't take any extra energy to double a recipe you are already making—and you get the double bonus of an additional meal to use on a busy day. *I put one in the oven or crock pot, and freeze the other.* I find that this is much less daunting for me than putting together a ton of meals in one day. I try to do at least one doubled recipe every week or so. This way I can stock up my freezer for those days when I just don't feel like cooking.

A Few Tips for a Big Freezer Meal Prep Day

#1 Double!!

I'm obviously a big fan of doubling recipes. This time I'm not cooking one meal and freezing the other, I'm simply making and freezing two of the same meal. Whenever I'm doing a big freezer meal day, I typically do this—at least with our very favorites. It's just so easy!! It takes no extra effort since it's all the same ingredients and prep. I do make sure to rotate the meals as I pull them out of the freezer. Also, this is a great way to share a meal with a friend who is in need of some TLC. Make a double recipe—one for yourself and another in a ziplock to take to a friend (be sure it has a label with instructions).

One little tip here: As you are doubling the recipe just make sure you are keeping track of which bowl or ziplock bag you are adding ingredients to. I accidentally added double the chili powder to a meal. I caught the mistake early and was able to dig it out before I combined the components. Could you imagine the surprise we would have had?

#2 Double bag your masterpieces.

This helps to protect you from unexpected leaks that can happen—and has happened to me—during the defrosting phase.

#3 Label!

I buy large labels that I can write the recipe name on—and the directions for cooking and ingredients to add (if not all are frozen). Putting the label on the outer bag is best, so that it can still be read if there is a leak. Again, I'm speaking from experience.

#4 Label or ziplock pantry items to be used in the meal.

I don't freeze every element of my freezer meal at times—especially if it's just broth or sauce that will fill up my freezer bag to capacity. Therefore, I've learned to label the items that were skipped. This saves me from accidentally using my last can of salsa or marinara sauce for a different recipe, if I know that it was purchased for one of my freezer meals. I sometimes create a little space on a pantry shelf to keep these extra ingredients. They also serve as a visual reminder that I have meals ready to go in the freezer.

#5 Extra copy!

Put an extra copy of the recipe in between the doubled freezer bags. I mainly do this when I'm delivering a meal to someone. I usually deliver meals hot and ready to eat, but sometimes I include an extra meal for them to toss in their freezer or refrigerator for another night.

#6 Make similar recipes at the same time.

If my main ingredient is ground beef in a few recipes, I cook up all the meat for the various recipes at the same time. This goes for chopping veggies and herbs, too. I often have several bags open that I'm tossing ingredients into. This tip works for chicken, too. In order not to confuse the bags, I put sticky notes on them (since I wait to put the official label on the outer bag). This helps me to keep track of what's going into each bag.

"FM2CP:" Freezer Meal to Crock Pot!

What could be better than creating freezer meals that go straight into your crock pot? There are actually recipes that can be frozen and then put in the crock pot. Double bonus! I put together a post of my Top 10 Freezer Meal 2 Crock Pot Recipes. I hope you'll love them as much as we do. We are usually making at least one of these recipes each week. They are our family's favorites.

Other Resources:

- **Posts**
  —Weekly Meal Planner and Grocery List: I share all my best meal planning tips and tricks here on this post, "Top 10 Freezer Meal 2 Crock Pot Recipes".

- **Books**
  —*Not Your Mother's Make-Ahead and Freeze Cookbook* by Jessica Fisher is a wonderful book for learning more about making freezer meals and is full of great recipes.

  —Crock On! A Semi-Whole Foods Slow Cooker Cookbook by Stacy Myers is an awesome cookbook with lots of great recipes, too.

- **Pinterest**
  —Food Yums! Crock Pot Recipes

  —Food Yums! Freezer Meals

- **My Meal Planner**
  —I'm so excited to share my "handy-dandy" meal planners with you. The planner is

available in black and white, as well as color, at the end of this book.

- **My FreezEasy Plan**
  —My friend, Erin Chase, created this really awesome freezer meal program. Be sure to check it out. It's really cool.

Again, links to all these resources (& more) can be found at:

KristiClover.com/SanitySaversResources

◎ Chapter Six ◎

SANITY SAVER #6

Create Your Own "Quiet Time!"

It's important for moms to re-boot their systems. As moms we are always serving. That's okay. I've learned that this is a beautiful gift I am giving my family. However, in order to best serve my family and the people the Lord brings into my life, I need to get breaks and some time for rest and rejuvenation.

We need to *make time* to relax! Schedule it in wherever we can! I purposely have a two-hour window for "quiet time" around 2pm. I put my little kids down for naps and quiet time—and take a deep breath. During this quiet time, my older kids may play basketball outside or read inside. Now, you do need to know that I am rarely able to get the full two hours of down time—but I'll take whatever I can get for each day. I have lots of "jack-in-the-box" kids, so I'm often spending much of my quiet time in the afternoon telling them to go back to their rooms. Really, all I want most days is just a little bit of time to be able to finish a thought without being interrupted.

Bedtimes are another key to quiet for me. I'm a firm believer in set bedtimes for my kids. We've always tried to get our kids to bed at a reasonable time so that we can have some quiet in the evenings. This is getting harder now that my boys are getting older. Sometimes they get home from basketball practice or youth group after the littles are in bed. I try to be patient and cherish the time to chat with them as they tell me how things went and grab a snack (since they never seem to be filled). But I'll admit, there is a part of me that is screaming, "This is my time! Go to bed!" I have to fight that feeling, but it's real. The nights they are home, they stay in their room and read after "bedtime" for the littles. This allows my husband and I some time alone to unwind from our day.

There is wisdom in the age-old saying of "when the baby rests, mama rests." Whether they are napping, just down for a quiet time, or to bed for the night, take time to relax a bit and catch your breath, read a book, call a friend, whatever you can do to re-energize—and maybe sneak in some extra time in the Word.

Another tip to get a little break in your day is to enlist the help of a friend. Swap babysitting for each other. This way you get a little break, then she gets a little break. It's a win-win!

We all need help sometimes—no matter what season of life we are in! What's crazy is that most of us hate asking for help, even though most moms love helping other moms! What stands in our way? Well, often it's pride, insecurity—or just complete exhaustion.

I remember several years ago having a breaking moment. We were at our homeschool co-op, and I was nursing our fourth little one during the moms' prayer time. We broke up into groups to pray just before we had to go and pick up our kids from their classes. Most of the time I would plaster a smile on my face and put my best foot forward. But this time, I was just tired. Too tired to care about what other moms might think.

So, I decided to ask for "prayer." I figured this was a good start. I wasn't asking for help, just for prayer. Well, God blessed me that day. My sweet friend, whom I was sitting with, offered to ask her daughter if she'd be willing to come over and help out. Not only was her daughter saving up for a ballet camp and looking for ways to earn some extra money, but we discovered that they lived three minutes away from me. Amazing! We ended up having this lovely, young lady come once a week for several months to help out.

Words cannot express how much that helped and blessed us. I learned such a valuable lesson that day! *Asking for help is sometimes the first step in allowing God to answer our prayer for help.* If it is pride that's getting in our way, we need to put it aside "and stop trying to impress others" (Philippians 2:3). Nobody really expects you to have it all together all the time. No one has mothering mastered. I have joked with friends about the fact that I'm just trying to "bless them with my mess." Ha! I do know that sometimes it's not about "impressing others" as much as we just don't want to scare anyone with our chaos.

Asking for help is sometimes the first step in allowing God to answer our prayer for help.

All that being said, all of us moms need to stick together! We need to unite. We need to draw on each other's strengths, not be intimidated by them. We need to get in the habit of checking in with each other to see if we can help each other out. All of us need breaks—and we also need fellowship and camaraderie! So, be sure to schedule in some girl time.

We all need a little "quiet" at some point in our ~~day~~ week. {I'm being real—it's sometimes hard to get quiet everyday. That's the goal, but I thought I'd say "week" there to make you feel better if it's not happening daily.} *So, let's work together and encourage one another to fill up our "sanity tanks" by being intentional about getting a little quiet into our lives.*

Other Resources:

- **Posts**
    —Daily Laying Down Your Life

    —M.O.M. Rule # 7: Ask for Help!

- **Books**
    —*Say Good-Bye to Survival Mode*
    by Crystal Paine

    —*Life Management for Busy Women*
    by Elizabeth George

* Links to all these resources can be found at:

KristiClover.com/SanitySaversResources

◎ *Chapter Seven* ◎

SANITY SAVER #7

Have Fun!

Nothing brings more sanity than having fun! It's important to *schedule time* with your husband, your kids—even with your extended family and friends. Sometimes it requires a bit of strategy— or as our family jokingly calls it "strategery." A little intentional planning and you are on your way to fun!

Fun creates memories—and laughter. Laughing is so good for you! The Bible tells us that <u>"a cheerful heart is good medicine"</u> (Prov. 17:22). The endorphins released from laugher help to relieve stress. So, let's talk fun and let the good times roll...

Intentional Fun

Fun isn't always spontaneous! *It's great when it happens this way, but I've found that I have to be very intentional about planning fun into our lives.* There are so many moving parts with our family of seven. Sometimes I have to be very strategic about clearing our calendar enough to allow time for fun. There are big trips that we take and put on the calendar, which are super fun. However, there are so many incredible things we can do right from home or in our area. It just takes a little planning.

Ready for my BEST tip on how to have fun? Make a list! I'm serious! I'm a list girl by nature, but fun will not happen in my house without my "Traditions" list and my "Family Fun" list. I don't know about you, but my mind often draws a blank when I have to come up with something exciting to do on the spot. There are weekends that we realize we don't have anything going on, and I can't think of a single thing to do. Often I'm just too tired from our busy week to come up with anything good. Granted, I personally think it is thrilling to gut a closet or reorganize the garage, but my family does not share this strange passion with me. Hence, the list.

I have been growing my lists for years. I mean, YEARS! I could write an entire book about creating family traditions, so I'll just give you a simple overview here. *The important thing to remember about making your own list is to keep it handy so you can always reference it and keep adding to it.* I don't care if you are a paper-girl or a digital-girl, just create a list on something. When I hear about someplace fun my friends went to over the weekend, a great new restaurant to try, a new twist on a holiday tradition—I write it down.

To create your own lists, simply sit down and create a few categories and start filling things in. I've created a few fun, little printables to get you started at the back of this book.

Traditions List

My "Traditions" list is categorized by month with the corresponding holiday traditions listed as well. I also have a spot for birthday traditions, along with party ideas. Something I've added recently to my Traditions list are the subcategories "Prep Needed" & "Annual Photos" to each month and tradition. This helps me to remember what tools, supplies, or plans I need to pull together to make our fun come alive for that tradition. I also try to get similar pictures for each tradition.

The great thing about getting the same or similar pictures each year is that you get to look back and see how much everyone has grown. I realize that this is true of any photos from the past year. However, it's so special to see everyone in the same position doing the same thing each year.

What are some of our annual photos? We always take a family photo in front of the tree on Christmas morning in our PJs. I also take a photo of the kids laying down on the floor in a star formation in their PJs (heads together). For birthdays we have a birthday cake hat that is required attire for the birthday girl or boy for most photos. Every summer I get a picture of the kids in the jacuzzi with my husband. There are some traditional photos that have gaps in the years. I used to get pictures of the kids with fall foliage each year—but I've missed a few years.

Family Fun List

As for my "Family Fun" list, I have lots of categories: Date Nights, Backyard Activities, Indoor Activities, Family Fun Nights, Theme Day Ideas, Fun Foods, Day Trip Ideas, Local Attractions, Fun Websites that have great ideas—just about anything I can think of or have heard about goes on this list. It started as just one big list, but I've added the sections to make it easier for me to find things whenever we are looking for something specific to do.

Fun doesn't have to be extravagant! Sometimes just planning a simple game night is just the perfect way to add some fun. We have a few favorite, family-friendly comedians we enjoy watching together to get the endorphins going. My seven year old has decided he wants to be a comedian and usually reenacts a few of the sketches—his version gets us laughing even more. Some nights we "pump up the volume," turn on some music, and have dance parties. My husband and I show off our 90's dance moves and laugh as the kids try to do them—like the night they tried to do "the worm" and looked like a bunch of fish out of water. I laugh just thinking about it.

Fun with your Priority Relationships!

Let me help you get your creative juices flowing with some fun ideas to add to your own Traditions and Family Fun lists. I created a few "fun" printables for you to get your own lists started (Ch. 9).

Your Spouse...

- **Plan date nights!** Date nights are a must when you are married, especially if you have kids! You need time away to escape the constant interruptions and distractions. Get a sitter or enlist the help of family or friends like we talked about in the last chapter. Just get out together as a couple!
- **Plan a weekend away together!** Again, it doesn't have to be extravagant! We've even had our kids stay with family and our "get-away" was in our own home. That was really fun!
- **Plan stay-at-home date nights!** Mark your calendars, get the kids to bed early, and have some fun at home together. We've done picnic desserts on the family room floor. Family Life has a great kit called "Simply Romantic Nights" that we've used for ideas. Be prepared to blush at a few of them. {It's linked at the end of this chapter and on my Resource Page.}
- **"Couple Time!"** Hmm? How to expand on this one? Let's just stay with the "make-you-blush" theme, and you'll know what I am suggesting. This is a vital part of your marriage. A great book for this area of your marriage is *Red Hot Monogamy* by Bill and Pam Farrel. I have to share my embarrassing story with you when I bought this book at a Christian bookstore. I didn't read

the title properly and thought it said *Red Hot "Monogram."* I don't know why I thought that or why I thought that would make a good read, but I chatted with the clerk about how it sounded like a great book and I couldn't wait to read it. Ha! I got home and *really* read the title—and just about died. I'm blushing now as I recall that day. All that to say, buy it online and save yourself the embarrassment.

- **Attend a marriage retreat!** We haven't been able to do this every year. We've only attended a few in our almost 19 years of marriage. However, they are always so great. Most churches host marriage retreats each year. If yours does not, then just check with some other churches in your area—and make a date. Another great retreat is Family Life's A Weekend to Remember.

- **Plan your own marriage seminar!** Several years ago we hosted a couple's group in our home. One of the things we went through was a DVD series by Mark Gungor called "Laugh Your Way to a Better Marriage." It was awesome. You don't have to do it in a group. In fact, there are two videos that were a little awkward to watch with other couples. Let's just say there was no discussion those nights, but we all knew what the homework assignment was.

- **Go through a good book together.** Most Christian bookstores have great books on marriage.

Your Kids...

- **Special Meals!** This is one of the simplest ways to get your kids excited. Who doesn't love a little "food fun?" Plan a color day and pick food that is only that color. You could plan a rainbow week by picking a different color for each day. Finish up your color week by making some yummy Lucky Charm Treats for the last day as a little Rainbow celebration. Homemade ice cream is a special treat in our home. So, sometimes I surprise them with a little ice-cream night. {It's been a while since we've done this one. If my kids read this, they are going to get on me about dusting off our ice-cream maker.}

- **Dude & Daughter Dates!** One-on-one time with your kids is so important, especially if you have a large family. My husband and I rotate taking kids out for special lunches or activities as much as possible. Sometimes, it's as simple as coffee or errands. We used to call these "dude dates" before we had the girls. Now, we've had to add "daughter dates" to the rotation. Whatever you call them—*getting your kids alone to connect with them and hear their heart is one of the best investments of your time.*

- **Themed Days!** We love theme days! I'll admit my older kids probably got to enjoy more of my creative, themed days than my younger ones now. This is a little reminder for me to start implementing some of the things on our "Family Fun" list. As for theme days, you can try a "Water

Day" which includes some fun "get wet" activities like water balloons, a homemade slip and slide, sprinklers, cut-up sponges, and fun pool activities. "Mini Olympics" are fun, too. There are lots of fun ideas for things to do with an Olympic theme on Pinterest. You can plan a "Messy Day" with shaving cream, finger paints, sidewalk chalk, and end the day with "Dirt Cake." {See my easy "Dirt Cake" below.} All of these activities are best during the summer when you can keep the mess outside.

- **Outdoor Fun!** Capture the flag, Nerf tag, flashlight tag at night—the list can go on. There are nights we just lay down and look at the stars. We also enjoy camping in our own backyard. Who needs a fancy vacation, when you can pitch a tent in your own yard—or living room? I guess that one doesn't qualify as being outdoors even though you are using outdoor equipment. Don't forget hikes, bikes, skates, and evening walks in the neighborhood. *It doesn't have to be complicated, it just has to be together.*

Special Note on Fun!

Take pictures!! You have to take pictures! I know I already talked about the traditional annual photos we take every year, but you need to take pictures of all the fun things you do. Don't be shy about asking strangers to snap a family picture. Nothing makes memories last longer than being able to look back at the photos you took. Making memories are so fun, but the bonus of pictures is that it takes you right back to that moment.

Basically, plan a family fun night. Go out and try something new. Just have fun, take pictures, and make memories as a family!

Other Resources:

- **Posts**
  —You can check out my blog for some posts on fun. I love sharing my fun ideas with my readers. The Lucky Charm Treats recipe is also linked on the resource page.

- **Books**
  —I have lots of great book recommendation both for having fun as a family and for strengthening your marriage on my resource page. Don't worry I linked the "Laugh Your Way to a Better Marriage" DVD series I mentioned here, too.

- **Websites**
  —Family Life! Check out their "Simply Romantic Nights" kit and their Weekend to Remember marriage retreat.

  —Celebrating Holidays! This is my friend Angie's amazing site with loads of fun tradition ideas and historical background information on our holidays:

  www.celebratingholidays.com

- **Dirt Cake Recipe...**

My "Dirt Cake" Recipe!

Be sure to make your "cake" in a small garden pot with a plastic flower in it. Also serve it with a trowel—& don't forget the gummy worms!

Ingredients:

- 1 bag of Oreos, crushed to look like dirt {I pulse them in my blender}
- 1 box of instant chocolate pudding, prepared according to directions
- 1 bag of Gummy worms (don't use the whole bag, just a few for fun)

Directions:

In your small garden pot, layer the crushed Oreos, chocolate pudding, then worms. Repeat the layering twice. Add a final layer of "dirt"—Oreos—to the top of your crazy creation. Stick a fake, plastic flower in the middle to make it look a bit more authentic. Set the trowel next to your creation. Depending on the size of your flower pot(s), you can make one big one and share it—or make small individual pots. Wait until you see their faces when you tell them that the flower arrangement is for dessert! Fun & yummy!

◎ Chapter Eight ◎

Conclusion:

Blessings & Joy

Motherhood is a journey. *It may feel like a never-ending marathon, but our time with our kids at home really does come to an end.* Our nest will be empty one day, so we need to make today count. I really want to be a mother with no regrets, yet I already have so many. I'm not perfect. I'm sure I'm loading my kids full of stories to tell their therapist someday.

Here's the thing—God can redeem our past mistakes! There is no greater gift we can give our kids than the example of humble repentance. I honestly think the more upfront we are about our shortcomings, the more we teach our kids about God's grace. Our kids see our sin! We lose our cool. We say the wrong things. We act unloving—and more I'm sure! *They see it!! Don't forget that! When you've messed up in front of your kids, you need to repent—to your kids!* The more they see how we handle the sin in our lives, the more they will learn and understand how to deal with and repent of the sin in their lives.

I want to leave a legacy of love, joy, kindness, and grace. Okay, I want all the fruits of the Spirit seen in my life—but for a mom who has struggled with anger, depression, and anxiety for years, this feels like a tall order. But I trust God to do a mighty work in me and in my mothering.

Now that my oldest son is a teenager and several inches taller than me, the reality that he will someday leave home hits me more and more with each passing day. I find myself hugging him every chance I get. I used to hate hearing moms with grown children tell me that "it goes so fast" when my boys were young and I felt exhausted from long days and lack of sleep. I hate to say that to you now, but it really is true.

I think one of the benefits of having a combination of older kids and younger kids in our home is that it has made me notice that my kids really are growing up—faster than I realized. It seems to have happened in the blink of an eye. I feel like I'm taking more time to slow down with my younger kids to really enjoy them while they are little. I'm even enjoying the crazy, toddler years with my youngest so much more than I ever did before, since I have a visual reminder with my other kids that they really do grow out of this stage. The seasons of sleepless nights, potty training, and even toddler tantrums pass. Granted, there are still tantrums when they get older. They just look different.

Life can be overwhelming. Days can be long. A full night's sleep may be a distant memory. Yet there is a gift in all of the crazy moments—the gift of motherhood. Hold tightly to it. Seek ways to bring more sanity to your days and to your family life. *I truly believe that as we seek the Lord and simplify all that we have going on—and treasure the time that we have—we will experience more joy.* **Enjoy the journey!**

Live Simply. Be Joyful.

◎ Chapter Nine ◎

Printables

"Sanity" Planners & Meal Planners

To jump start your "sanity" I created these fun printables for you. My hope it that they will help you start simplifying and organizing your thoughts.

"Sanity" Planners...

Morning Goals:

- Box #1 Write down your goals for the morning
- Box #2 Draw up your "plan of attack" to accomplish those goals. Be sure to check your calendar and figure out what time you'd like to try to fit your goals in.
- Box #3 Once you have figured out all you need for the next day in your "plan," it's time to start gathering things and putting everything out that you'll need for a smooth morning.

- Box #4 Figuring out a bedtime for myself made me feel a bit silly. However, after I started getting more sleep and feeling more refreshed, it no longer felt silly-it was necessary.

Daily Routines:

Take time to write down what you'd like to accomplish in all the different segments of your day. You can add time blocks next to each section, or not. You may find that things need to get moved around to actually get accomplished. That was the story with piano practice for us. I had it in the evenings and it was never getting done. So, it got moved to mornings and the kids have been much more consistent at practicing.

Fun Planner:

"Yay!" for fun! It really does sound strange to have to plan out fun, but I tell you we have more fun when we have a plan. I created this little printable for you to start writing some of your ideas down.

Traditions Planner:

I'm sure you will eventually outgrow this printable, but it will help you get all your thoughts in one place. You can always use the back of each page, if you'd like. The point is to get started with your intentional fun.

Meal Planners...

I love my meal planners! I'm excited to share them with you here. They are one of my most popular subscriber freebies on my blog. You can pick from the Color version or Black & White version. It's up to you and your color ink status.

Ready to Print?

I'd love for you to be able to actually "print" these fun printables. I have them available for you (and so much more) when you join my "Simply Joyful" community.

Go to:

KristiClover.com/SanitySaversPrintables

Sanity Savers for Moms: The Coloring Book

Yes, *Sanity Savers for Moms* has a coloring book! This fun, little coloring book is filled with quotes from the book and Bible verses to color and get your creative juices flowing. There are even clovers hidden on each page (some more obvious than others). Be sure to get this incredibly encouraging companion book to go with your *Sanity Savers* book. Everybody needs a little more sanity in their day — and taking time to color just might be the answer you're looking for!

Check it out at:

KristiClover.com/store

44882582R00047

Made in the USA
San Bernardino, CA
23 July 2019